Great Orders of the Catholic Church

From the Benedictines to the Carmelites

by

Harry Schnitker

All booklets are published thanks to the generous support of the members of the Catholic Truth Society

CATHOLIC TRUTH SOCIETY

PUBLISHERS TO THE HOLY SEE

Contents

ISBN 978 1 86082 917 8

Introduction

The religious life (a life vowed exclusively to God) has been a feature of the Church from very early in its history. Since the fourth century, men and women have lived in groups or alone to dedicate themselves to prayer and work. This movement began in Egypt and the Middle East, and from there has expanded across the globe. There are very few places in the world where there are no men or women in Catholic religious orders. From its early roots, the Church has seen an enormous multiplication of orders and movements. Some are very small, no more than a few men or women living together in community in a small house. Others are huge. They have provided the Church with many of her popes and cardinals, bishops, priests, teachers, spiritual guides, hospital staff, scientists and academics. Since 2013, they have once again, for the first time in almost two centuries, provided the Church with its leader: Pope Francis is a member of the Society of Jesus (or 'Jesuits').

In the pages that follow, some of the largest or most influential of these orders or religious families which have their roots in the period before the Reformation will be introduced. They are presented roughly in chronological sequence, so as to provide the reader with a sense of the development of the idea of the religious life. This began with a wish to retreat from the world and live in communion, gradually developed rules by which the religious could live, and expanded into organised movements. Later, the idea of mendicant groups, working in the world to meet its needs and challenges, arose.

Many medieval religious orders have managed to survive the impact of the Reformation, and the even sterner challenges of the French Revolutionary epoch, radical secularism, Communism and unbridled capitalism. Whenever it seemed that they were doomed to extinction, they began to flourish again, sometimes far from where they were started, at other times experiencing amazing resurrections where they had vanished. Even today, those orders of the Church with their roots in the medieval period contribute significantly to her mission.

In the global Church, the number of diocesan priests has been steadily rising over the past few decades. Many of the religious orders, on the other hand, have suffered a decline of varying proportions. The female religious, in particular, have seen vocations decline dramatically in many parts of the globe. It is hoped that this book will help in raising the awareness of what the orders have to offer, so that more people may feel the call to religious life.

The Benedictines

Origins

The Benedictines are the oldest continuous monastic movement in the Church. When St Benedict first started his monastic life in around AD 500, he met monks already living the solitary life in the mountains in Enfide, some fifty miles east of Rome. These were inspired by the monastic movements in Egypt and the Middle East, and were following a large variety of rules. Some lived the eremitical life (the life of hermits); others were coenobitic, living in community. However, through the Rule he wrote, Benedict placed monasticism on an organised footing.

There is much scholarly debate around the source for the life of St Benedict, *The Dialogues, Book II*. These were long held to have been written by Pope St Gregory the Great. That view has been challenged, but there is little doubt that Benedict was, indeed, an historical figure. Nor does one require the mythical elements of the *Dialogues* to write a broad outline of the early Benedictine movement.

The Benedictines took several centuries to become the dominant monastic movement. Although St Benedict founded several houses near Subiaco, and was Abbot of Monte Cassino when he died around AD 543, his cult was not fully developed until after 670. After that, it would take another century or so before most European monasteries adopted the Benedictine Rule. This was under the influence of the Emperor, Charlemagne (747-814), who saw the Holy Rule as a unifying element for the monasteries in his almost Europe-wide empire.

St Benedict's sister, St Scholastica, also lived the religious life, and from the start there has been a strong female component to the Benedictine movement. Like their male counterparts, the nuns were mainly contemplative. Their lives were a mixture of work to provide food and shelter, hospitality, prayer and *lectio divina*. Like the monks, the nuns contributed greatly to the life of the Church.

The centuries from the ninth to the twelfth are known as the Benedictine centuries. The monasteries became centres of learning and teaching, their libraries receptacles for the culture of Antiquity; they stood at the cradle of the liberal arts and of scientific research. It is no exaggeration to say that the Benedictines were crucial in the shaping of a European civilisation. Benedictine monks were great missionaries, and much credit must go to them for the conversion of Germany east of the Rhine, Scandinavia and Central Europe. All this time, there was no Benedictine order. Instead, each house constituted its own family.

Throughout their history, the Benedictines have undertaken numerous reform attempts. The first of the reforms came as the Holy Rule swept all before it in the eighth century. St Benedict of Aniane (c. 745-821) founded a great house on his ancestral estate in southern France, which became the loadstone for the monastic life in the Carolingian Empire. The first true congregation within the Benedictine movement came into being at Cluny in Burgundy. There, in 910, the Holy Rule was adapted to create a monastic culture centred on an elaborate celebration of the monastic hours and the liturgy. The Abbot of Cluny became the head of an order, which, at its peak, consisted of 310 houses spread across Europe. For two centuries, saintly abbots from Cluny shaped every aspect of religious life, and were instrumental in promoting the rise of Gothic architecture. Cluny was exempt from episcopal control, and exercised profound influence on the Papacy.

In the eleventh century, the Benedictines experienced renewed reform vigour. It began in Italy, where St Romuald (c. 951-c. 1027) founded the Camaldolese Hermits. This was an attempt to return to the eremitical ideals of the Egyptian desert. St John Gualbert (c. 985-1073), another Italian, founded Vallumbrosa. Whereas Romuald simply wished to introduce a new form of Benedictine-ism, Gualbert's foundation was a reaction against the corruption and lax morals of contemporary monasticism in Italy.

New monastic movements, some based on the Holy Rule, sprang up in this period of great religious revival, but the Benedictine movement continued with some vigour. The next great change took place after the Fourth Lateran Council, which, in 1215, passed legislation to maintain monastic standards. One of these was the decision to erect congregations. It is at this time that the first mention is made of 'St Benedict's Order'. The first country to accept this was England, where the English Benedictine Congregation was founded in the thirteenth century. National congregations were often the norm, as in Hungary, where a congregation was erected in 1514, or in Switzerland, where one came into being in 1602. Others were local, or organised around a mother abbey. Cluny was one example of the latter, the Bavarian Congregation, erected in 1684, of the former. Some have had a very long life, others were cut short by wars, revolutions or anti-clericalism, like the Portuguese Congregation.

In some countries, like England and Scotland, much of the Low Countries, Scandinavia and large swathes of Germany, many Benedictine houses were closed during the Reformation. This followed closely on serious reform attempts, such as the Congregation of Bursfeld, which, nevertheless, proved insufficient. Benedictine life continued, and it is in the seventeenth century that the word 'Benedictine' makes its first appearance. The Benedictines were particularly hard hit by the French Revolutionary epoch. The renowned Congregation of St Maur, which had contributed so significantly to the Enlightenment, received as little mercy as the small houses still clustered around Europe. Even Cluny, which had survived for eight centuries, was closed.

By 1820, only some thirty houses survived. There followed a great revival of the Benedictine ideal, sometimes referred to as the Second Benedictine Flowering. Amongst the most significant congregations were Solesmes in France, founded in 1833 by Dom Prosper Guérenger, which made a significant contribution to plainchant; Subiaco in Italy (1851) and Beuron in Germany (1863). Missionary activity expanded the Benedictines across the globe, with major congregations in the United States, Brazil, and large houses in Africa and Asia. Benedictine sisters came into being, dedicated to health care or work in the mission, and, in 1893, Pope Leo XIII united the disparate Benedictines into a confederation.

Since the Second Vatican Council there has been a decline in numbers, but an expansion into wider society. The oblate movement has brought lay people in contact with monasteries and the Holy Rule, and many monasteries now have large numbers of oblates living the Benedictine life within the world. The Holy Rule has been adapted for management, and there are Benedictine leadership courses.

Important Benedictines

In a movement that has spanned over fifteen hundred years, it is difficult to choose the most important figures: for everyone included here there are at least ten others! The most obvious are Saints Benedict and Scholastica. Unfortunately, almost all we know about them comes from *The Dialogues, Book II*, and its trustworthiness has been called into question. However, if we can say little about Scholastica, then the Holy Rule contains enough personal touches to allow us to say something about Benedict. He was a man who above all loved peace, which is the motto of many a Benedictine abbey. He was considerate and did not make exorbitant demands from his monks. Benedict also placed a heavy obligation of care and compassion on the abbot and prior. Above all, he wished the community to worship God. It is, therefore, appropriate that he reputedly died while standing in prayer in the church of Monte Cassino.

The English Benedictine, St Bede (672-735), is an excellent example of Benedictine learning. He was a monk at Jarrow in Northumberland, where he was educated from the age of seven. He entered the monastery as a monk, and there wrote over sixty books, including the *Ecclesiastical History of the English-Speaking Peoples*. The latter was the first to consider the various Anglo-Saxons in Britain as one people. Bede was a great teacher as well as writer, and the monastery was a centre of educational excellence. From his writings it is clear that there was an extensive library at Jarrow, and Bede's life is a perfect illustration of the Benedictine impact on European civilisation. Bede is best known for standardising the usages of 'BC' and 'AD', thus effectively Christianising time itself.

St Romuald, founder of the Camaldolese Hermits, has already been mentioned. Not only was his life a great example of religious fervour, but he was also a typical charismatic monastic and an important contributor to the spiritual life. It is his focus on contemplation that makes him stand out. One can do no better than to quote the advice to his monks:

> "Sit in your cell like in paradise. Watch your thoughts as fishermen watch fish. The path you must follow is the Psalms - never leave it. Realise above all that you are in God's presence...empty yourself completely and sit waiting, content with the Grace of God".

Romuald's hermits followed a quietist path that echoed through time, and crossed denominational and religious boundaries.

Amongst the many outstanding Benedictine females, St Frances of Rome (1384-1440) may be mentioned. Frances was married against her wishes, but loved and supported her husband, Lorenzo, through a forty-year marriage. Lorenzo died in 1436, having suffered for years from wounds received in war. In a troubled Rome, Frances opened her house to the sick and suffering, strengthened by her mystic faith. In 1433, she and those helping her turned her house into a community, given oblate status by Pope Eugene IV. Frances was, in turn, wife, mother, mystic, nurse, friend and religious. Through all of these stages, the Holy Rule was her guide and companion. Canonised, she is now the patron of all Benedictine oblates.

Charism and Spirituality

The Holy Rule is the basis of Benedictine life. It is based on an older monastic Rule, *The Rule of the Master*, which St Benedict altered significantly. The Holy Rule consists of two main elements: worship and community life. The monastery is presented as school, which will lead the monk or nun to a regulated life of work and prayer, and through this to peace.

A major component of the Rule concerns the liturgy, and in particular the singing of the Psalms. These form the mainstay of the Benedictine life, and through a life-long contemplation of the Psalms one is led to a perfect understanding of God. Through the Psalms, the monastic life is totally Christ-centred.

There is a warmth of feeling in the Rule, which made it stand out when it was written. Superiors are admonished to care for their flock, and all are made aware of the need of a proper humility and appropriate obedience. Yet human frailty is respected, and there are many exceptions made for the sick, the infirm and the young and old. For many centuries, it has been the bedrock of Western monasticism, and is in use in Benedictine, Cistercian, Trappist and Mekhtarist houses. Surprisingly, it has also become popular outside the monastery, and now guides the lives of thousands of oblates.

The Augustinians

Occasionally, it is still claimed that the Augustinians originated in the fourth century. It is true that St Augustine lived in community after his baptism in AD 385, and that he wrote his letter No. 122 for his monastic sister, which would become the Rule of St Augustine. That Rule, however, was lost and rediscovered only in the late eleventh century. This caused a shock-wave amongst the religious in Europe. The Gregorian reform movement had long claimed that since the apostles lived like monks, all clergy should be like monks.

As a result, many clergy had adopted a monastic life without withdrawing from the world. They were known as Canons Regular, but had no common Rule. St Peter Damian (c. 1007-1073) had written instructions for some of these communities, but it was the rediscovery of St Augustine's Rule that would provide them with their foundation stone. It soon came to be the Rule for Canons Regular, for the Order of Prémontré and for the Dominican friars. As C.H. Lawrence observed, it was often difficult to see the difference between Benedictine houses and those of the Canons Regular. Perhaps the main difference lay in the emphasis on study rather than manual work, and in the more generous dietary allowances given to the canons. Some movements were, however, very severe, such as those of St Victor or Arrousaise.

Popes tried to ensure a proper understanding of the distinction between Benedictines and Augustinian canons. Urban II wrote that whereas monks resembled Mary, canons took the role of Martha. This focused minds, and soon the manifold orders of Augustinian Canons Regular were found in many cathedrals, as well as in monastic houses. Over time, they would become more numerous than the Benedictines. Many houses served as hospitals for the sick, the old and for pilgrims. Amongst the most famous of these are the Abbey of St Maurice of Agaune and the Hospice of St Bernard of Mont-Joux, both in Switzerland. Women, too, became canonesses, but their role was mainly contemplative, and they never reached the same prominence as the canons.

Some canons went beyond the traditional role. The Order of Prémontré, founded by St Norbert of Xanten (c. 1080-1134), is the most famous example. Its houses were in remote places, and they concerned themselves more with the sanctification of the canons than with any outside commitments. It was not until much later that these canons would take up their active life again. Again, the order has a female branch, which is still mainly contemplative. Over time, the Canons Regular would produce some of the greatest figures of medieval

Christendom. These include several popes, but also the most influential spiritual writer that Catholicism ever produced, Thomas à Kempis, whose *Imitation of Christ* is outsold only by the Bible. À Kempis belonged to the *Devotio Moderna* or Windesheimer Congregation.

Like the Benedictines, the Canons Regular came to be organised around congregations, many of which did not survive the upheavals of the Reformation or the French Revolutionary period. In some countries, like Austria, they survived in numbers, in others they have been revived on many occasions. They were united in a confederation by Pope St John XXIII in 1959. The Order of Prémontré, also known as Norbertines, as well as the Crosiers, the Lateran Congregation and the Canons of the Immaculate Conception, have all remained outside the confederation.

The Augustinian family soon extended beyond the Canons Regular. In the early thirteenth century, several communities of hermits in central Italy united. They sought a common Rule, and in 1231 Pope Gregory IX granted them the Rule of St Augustine. Alexander IV summoned all the various eremitical communities to Rome in 1256, and, in the Magna Unio, enrolled them in a single order, the Hermits of St Augustine, who are friars or mendicants. The many communities of nuns following the Rule at this point were not consolidated into a single order. Many engaged in close association with the hermits from the fifteenth century onwards.

They were active in the life of the Church from early on, and were instrumental in the development of the use of the printing press to disseminate Catholic teaching. The Reformation hit the order hard. Martin Luther was an Augustinian hermit, but this did not prevent the closure of numerous houses. As the Old World closed many doors, the New World opened them. Augustinians were particularly prominent in the Portuguese missions in Africa, as well as in Spanish missions in Latin America and in the Philippines. In most countries, they were the first priests to work there.

It is simply impossible to consider all the various orders that are part of the Augustinian family today in such a short space. Amongst the better-known orders to have adopted the Rule are the Servites, founded in Italy in 1233 and one of the original mendicant orders of the Church, the Mercedarians, founded in Spain in 1218 to ransom captives from the Muslims, and the Order of St Paul the First Hermit, founded in Hungary in 1250. The hermits have witnessed several reform movements, including the Recollects, founded in 1621, and the Discalced Augustinians, founded in 1610, both created as part of the Catholic Reformation. Augustinian lay societies have sprung up in the past century or so.

Amongst female religious orders using the Rule, the Ursulines may be noted. There are several Ursuline orders, and only the enclosed ones follow the Rule. The movement was begun by St Angela Merici in Italy in 1535. It grew into one of the largest teaching movements in the Church, and the Ursulines were the first female religious order in North America. Supported by St Charles Borromeo and St Frances de Sales, their impact on the education of women has been profound.

Important Augustinians

As for the Benedictines it is impossible to do justice to all prominent Augustinians in such short space. St Augustine (354-430), the author of the core of the Rule, is well known. He is a Doctor of the Church and one of the Latin Church Fathers. His troubled youth, slow conversion of the faith and tragic life of loss all substantially influenced his theology. He is, of course, much better known for his theology of grace and original sin than he is as the author of a monastic Rule. However, his own conversion came through the reading of the life of the father of monasticism, St Anthony. The resulting *Confessions*, his autobiographical account of his journey to faith, has been instrumental in converting thousands ever since.

Augustine's influence on so many people was profound. We have encountered St Norbert of Xanten above, and he may be seen as typical of those who were inspired by the Rule to create religious communities. Norbert was a nobleman, connected to the German Imperial family, who gave his estates away after a religious conversion. He was a great ascetic, who was commissioned as an itinerant preacher by Pope Gelasius II. On his travels, he noted the many demoralised diocesan priests, living lives of loneliness, alleviated by concubines. This convinced him of the need for communal living. In answer, he founded a new house in Prémontré, from where the new Norbertine order grew. His canons were frequently very Cistercian in their mode of living. By the mid-fourteenth century, there were some fourteen hundred houses for men and four hundred for women.

Perhaps the most famous of all Augustinians is St Rita of Cascia (1381-1457). Like St Frances of Rome, her husband fell victim to the violence of the era; her children died of disease. Unlike St Frances, her marriage was marked by abuse. After her losses, she joined an Augustinian community, after being rejected for some considerable time. There, she proved to be blessed by intense religious visions, and an ability to maintain the peace between various factions in the house. She became known for her powerful intercession, and is a patron for abused women.

Famous, too, is Martin Luther. Indeed, he is possibly the most famous Augustinian of all. The reformer, whom Benedict XVI argued was frequently misunderstood, had fully absorbed the writings of St Augustine, and was an avid student of his theology of grace and original sin. Of course, he famously claimed to have entered the order for false motives. Luther insisted on the invalidity of the religious life, but it survived.

As the Church expanded, in Japan the impact of the Augustinians was profound. They first arrived in 1602, but twelve years later faced fierce persecution. The Augustinians had converted many Japanese, and had brought missionaries to Japan from all over the Catholic world. This shows in the list of martyrs. The proto-martyrs were Spaniard, Fr Ferdinand of St Joseph, and Japanese catechist, Andrew Yoshida. Others came from Mexico, like Fr Peter Zúñiga, but the majority were Japanese. Some were Augustinians and wished to leave, other suffered and stayed faithful.

Others yet managed to live the religious life whilst at the same time contributing significantly to the scientific understanding of the world. Gregor Mendel (1822-1884) was both an Augustinian monk and the pioneer scientist in genetics. Mendel came from a rural background in what is now the Czech Republic. He entered the Augustinians on the advice of his science teacher - his abbot sent him to Vienna to study sciences! In the monastery, he kept a large number of bees which he bred for improved resistance to disease and greater tolerance of poor weather. Mendel was aware that certain desirable strains were inherited from individual queens. It was not until after 1900 that Mendel's works were rediscovered. He is now seen as the father of modern genetics, and, in many ways, as profound a contributor to our understanding of the natural world as Darwin.

Charism and Spirituality

Arguably the most essential element in the Rule of St Augustine is brotherhood. Where Benedict saw the monastic life as a proofing ground for individuals living in community, Augustine saw it as a place where God and fellow men could be served. This had a purpose: he wished to create a harmonious community intent on worshipping God. The end-result of both ancient rules, then, was the same, but the emphasis was quite different.

The equality of all, implicit with Benedict, is made explicit by Augustine: “The rich…who seemed important in the world, must not look down upon their brothers who have come into this holy brotherhood from a condition of poverty. They should seek to glory in the fellowship of poor brothers”. Work, too, is in the service of others. Charity, Augustine stated, meant greater concern for the common good than for one’s own. Great emphasis is placed on the care of the sick and the infirm, as well as of those incapacitated. Indeed, the Rule has been called the earliest post-Scriptural social document of the Church.

The Cistercians

Of all the reform movements in the Church, the greatest was undoubtedly that centred on Cîteaux. We have already seen that the Benedictines were characterised by frequent waves of reform. One of these occurred on 21st March 1098, when Robert, Abbot of Molesme, and twenty-one companion monks left their abbey and wandered off into the wilderness. They had given up their attempt to introduce a rigid reform of the Holy Rule at Molesme, and were now striking out for themselves.

It was an exodus with enormous consequences for the spiritual life of the Church. The earliest Cistercians followed a most rigorous version of the Holy Rule, stripped of all the liturgical and artistic encrustations that the mainstream Benedictines, and in particular Cluny, had developed. St Robert was succeeded by two more saints as leaders of the new house. St Alberic, who adopted the white habit that would come to characterise the Cistercians, was deeply devoted to Mary. It was a devotion shared by all who were to follow him: a deep love of Mary would characterise the Cistercians, who would name all their houses after the Mother of God.

St Stephen Harding, the third abbot, was an Englishman. He was the organisational genius whose deft touch in managing people and creating structures enabled the phenomenal growth of the new order. That this happened was providential. For the first decade and more, the new foundation at Cîteaux floundered, and its monks suffered great hardships. Then, in 1112, came the man who would shape the Cistercians: St Bernard of Clairvaux.

St Bernard came to Cîteaux with thirty fellow monks, most of them his relatives. Three years later, he was sent to create a new house at Clairvaux. There followed a quite extra-ordinary flourishing of the monastic life. By the end of the thirteenth century, Europe had over five hundred Cistercian monasteries: the greatest monastic order of the Middle Ages was born. The Cistercians returned to the monastic ideal of the desert. Houses were founded in the wilderness, where monks did hard work instead of study. We are told that Caesarius of Heisterbach (1180-1240), author of the *Dialogus miraculorum*, that great bestseller of the Middle Ages, was attracted to the Cistercians by a story of how Our Lady, with St Anne and St Mary Magdalen joined choir monks and lay brothers as they worked to reap the harvest at Clairvaux.

The Cistercians cultivated what C.H. Lawrence called a "cult of poverty". The habit was coarse and simple, the food, exceedingly plain, privacy, unknown. They also created a whole new architecture, characterised by simple, unadorned churches and monasteries, stark arcades and no carvings. It was to have a deep influence on nineteenth and twentieth century Modernism.

The movement attracted women, too. A first house was opened in 1125, with nuns from the Abbey of Jully. It was established at Tart, and its first abbess was St Humbeline, sister to St Bernard of Clairvaux. Soon, the new nuns attracted whole Benedictine houses, and even congregations. The apogee was reached in 1180, with the royal foundation of the Abbey of Las Huelgas.

Of course, the total renunciation of all possessions was impossible to maintain. Ironically, the Cistercians' great success as farmers, breaking in waste all over Europe, created an impossible contradiction: their agrarian enterprises, including large-scale sheep-farming and the construction of large water mills, brought great wealth to the Cistercian houses. Lay brothers, considered of a lower status than the choir monks, soon took over all the work, whilst the choir monks lived a life more akin to that of the Benedictines of Cluny. However, the ideal remained as a powerful idea.

The later Middle Ages and Reformation were not kind to the Cistercians. Their great wealth made them obvious targets for greedy monarchs, their own lax morals laying them open to justified accusations of improper behaviour. The foundation of congregations, like the early Congregation of Castile (1425), helped a little, but could not prevent decline. It was not until the seventeenth century that successful reform movements arose within the Cistercians. Only that begun by Armand Jean le Bouthillier de Rancé (1626-1700) at La Trappe had lasting success. The Cistercians of the Strict Observance, better known as Trappists, returned to the early ideal of St Robert of Molesme and his monks.

This time, the reform lasted, and the Trappists are, to this day, characterised by great simplicity and austerity. Such was its reputation, that the earliest monks at La Trappe called themselves prisoners of Christ. The order was hit hard by the French Revolution, but bounced back with verve in the nineteenth century. It has a pronounced presence all over the British Isles, from Caldey in Wales to Nunraw in Scotland, and from Mount St Bernard in England to New Melleray in Ireland.

Both branches of the Cistercian family now maintain close contacts. The older one has declined significantly in many parts of Europe, but has maintained a presence in countries like Austria, Poland and Spain. In addition, Cistercian life is flourishing in south-east Asia. The Trappists have managed to survive in countries where the Church has been hard hit by secularisation, like the Benelux, France and the Czech Republic. Vocations are down, but not as radically as for many other orders. Elsewhere, they have expanded in Latin America, Asia and Africa.

Important Cistercians

There is little doubt that *the* outstanding Cistercian is St Bernard of Clairvaux (1090-1153). Bernard was the son of Burgundian high nobility, who developed a precocious interest in literature and poetry. This was, at the time, a highly secular pursuit, for this was the era of courtly love troubadours. For Bernard, however, literature was a means of studying Scripture, the traditions of courtly love a tool for reinterpreting the Gospels. His mother died when he was only nineteen, and Bernard, whose life was not free from temptations at this point, decided to enter the religious life. We have already encountered his role in the creation of the Cistercian order, and it was whilst occupied with this that Bernard refined his own vision of love, and in particular love in the Gospels. His firm devotion to Our Lady helped him to envisage love as the essential cornerstone in the relation between human beings and God. He established firmly the importance of the emotive element of faith, deeming it to be of far more consequence than any rational approach.

Bernard was frequently disliked by the Church's hierarchy, and was once referred to as a "noisy and troublesome frog" by an irritated cardinal. However, gradually his influence increased, and Bernard was to have the ear of popes. He was often offered high ecclesiastical office, but always refused: Bernard was a Cistercian monk, nothing else.

There have been many important Cistercians since St Bernard, but for contemporary influence none has matched the great American Trappist, Thomas Merton (1915-1968). Born in France to a New Zealand father and American Mother, Merton was brought up an Anglican. They soon moved to the United States. In his early years, his father was normally absent. Merton lost his mother when he was aged only six, and shared this early loss of maternal influences with St Bernard. In 1926, he was sent to a French boarding-school, which filled Merton with loathing and loneliness. He lacked any sense of faith, and displayed a strong relativism.

He moved to an English boarding-school, and, in 1931, he lost his father. Three years later, and about to enter Cambridge, he visited Rome. There, he had an extraordinary experience: he visited Tre Fontene, the Trappist monastery in Rome, and knew that he wanted to become a monk. At this point, he was a profound agnostic, with a reputation for rather loose living. His stint at Cambridge, and then at Columbia University, was marked by several relations with women, and a total lack of interest in anything religious. Towards the late 1930s, however, he began to read medieval philosophy and medieval French literature, and drifted towards Catholicism. A reading of St Augustine's *Confessions* and the *Imitation of Christ* intensified this shift. In 1938, he was baptised a Catholic, joined the peace movement and *Catholic Action*, and began testing a vocation.

Neither the diocesesan priesthood nor the Franciscans could hold Merton's attention, but a retreat at Gethsemani Abbey re-kindled his first inclination, felt in Rome in 1933, for the Trappist life. It would not be until 1942 that he was finally allowed to enter Gethsemani. His twenty-six years at the abbey were to see him become a household name, and not just in Catholic circles. Merton's powerful prose and poetry speaks of love for God and the perfect silence of the monastery, of the human need for contemplation, and of the beauty of the religious life.

Charism and Spirituality

The Cistercian's core principles can be summed up in two words: love and sobriety. Of the two, the latter has caused most comments. First the Cistercians, and then the Trappists were renowned for their abstinence from many sources of food, and the reduction of their possessions to the bare minimum. In its more extreme forms, this was suited only to a monastic setting. However, the emphasis on the preciousness of every object, the rejection of acquiring more than is needed to live and the rejection of worldly success is perfectly applicable outside the monastery.

There is a solid reason for this rejection: as the Carta Caritatis or Charter of Charity, the foundational document of the order, puts it, "lest striving to be made wealthy from their poverty, we may incur the guilt of vice and avarice, which the apostle terms the 'serving of idols'". Vice and avarice are sins to God, but also to others, and solidarity is, as we have seen, a cornerstone of the Holy Rule that the Cistercians wished to restore.

Love is seldom associated with the Cistercians or Trappists, but it is the most important principle underpinning the order. St Bernard was clear that it was God's love of humanity that caused the Incarnation, and that her love for fellow human beings made Mary the Mediatrix between humanity and God.

The Carthusians

Like the Cistercians, the Carthusians were part of the great zeal for reform that characterised the eleventh century. Unlike the Cistercians, or the Camaldolese or Vallumbrosians, the new order was not simply based on a modification of the interpretation of the Holy Rule of St Benedict. Instead, it was the only lasting attempt to renew the ancient Palestinian monastic ideal of the *lavra*, the eremitical community. This is, of course, a contradiction in terms, but was effectively a model which allowed contemplatives to live in isolation without losing the advantages of communal worship. The Camaldolese had also grown from this notion, but, as seen, they based their lives on the Holy Rule, which stated that the eremitical life was the apogee of the monastic ideal.

The man responsible for introducing the first truly new monastic family in the Latin Church since the eighth century was St Bruno Hartenfaust (c. 1030-1101). His life will be considered below. For now, it is sufficient to relate here that he withdrew from a particularly active life within the Church to the wilderness of La Chartreuse, in the French Alps, in 1084. He attracted only a few followers, who lived in great privation. The climate at La Chartreuse is harsh, with snow lying on the ground for many months. In 1084, it was also spectacularly remote. Lodged in individual cells, the monks spent long hours in total isolation, concentrating on a rigid prayer-life centred on the Liturgical Hours. Somehow, they managed to survive for six years.

With Bruno called to Rome by Pope Urban II to assist him in furthering the wider reform of the Church, the community rapidly fell apart, only to reform and begin on a slow route to growth. Bruno would found a second house in southern Italy, where he was in exile with Urban II during one of those uncountable episodes of violence on the peninsula in which the Papacy was wont to get caught up. This was at La Torre, a house which was not quite as successful as La Chartreuse. Bruno died in 1101, leaving behind only two houses. When compared to the great reform movements of Cluny, Prémontré or Cîteaux, it was a pitifully small achievement, unlikely to survive and unlikely to become of any consequence at any level but the purely local.

The real growth of this most austere of orders did not commence until after its founder's death. That is of interest, for it goes against the normal trend. Bruno was most certainly a charismatic figure, and his impact on the Carthusians is profound. Yet he was no St Bernard, no St Norbert. Instead, it was the ideal which he had expounded that flourished, and ideals survive much better than the charisma of individuals. In 1128, the *Consuetudines*

Cartusiae were written, providing the order with its own Rule. The monopoly of the Rule of St Benedict was broken. Written, according to tradition, by Guigues, one of St Bruno's successors, it was firmly based on Carthusian tradition and harked back to the original instructions by St Bruno. It provided the spiritual basis for the new order, of which more anon, but also gave it a structure.

Each Charterhouse, as the monasteries are called, was to have thirteen hermit-monks, each living in his own small house with a garden. There are also a number of lay brothers, whose liturgical duties are slightly less intense than those of the monks, but who express their spirituality through work for the common good. All were to live lives of isolation, the lay brothers less so than the monks. All were to eat and drink alone, sleep little and work hard. It was a highly regulated life, but one that obviously appealed to a segment of those wishing to embrace the religious life.

Within a century, a further thirty-three Charterhouses were founded including several in England. In 1147, religious sisters began to affiliate themselves with the Carthusians, creating the first order of female hermits in the Latin Church. By 1260, their numbers had grown to nine houses and some hundred nuns.

The order reached its greatest extent and influence between 1350 and 1550. The relentless drive for spiritual perfection, and the deeply democratic spirit of the order (it does not have abbots but just priors) ensured that it did not suffer from some of the corruptions that marred the religious life in other orders. This, in turn, ensured that pious lay people supported the order financially, including many monarchs across Europe. Even the death of some nine hundred monks and lay brothers during the Black Death did not impact on the order's growth, or on the spiritual purity of the Carthusians.

At its height in 1514, the order had 196 Charterhouses in every corner of Europe. The Reformation hit them hard, as many houses were singled out by Protestants as being the most likely source of opposition. The Charterhouse in Perth, in Scotland, for example, was the first religious house in that country to be burnt down. In England, eighteen Carthusians were savagely martyred, and another thirty-two followed on the Continent. There is something particularly shocking about their martyrdoms, for these were men whose lives were spent away from the world in prayer and contemplation. The Charterhouses were not particularly rich, and the order had not imposed itself on wider society, as had become the case with some others.

The seventeenth century saw a revival with the foundation of twenty-one new houses, and by 1676 it achieved its largest contingent of monks and nuns: 1,500 and 120 respectively. Again, they were hit hard by the secularism and atheism of the next century. During the French Revolution, another fifty monks and at least five nuns were martyred, and by 1810 there were only eight

Charterhouses left, with no female foundations at all. From this deep trough, the order revived. Although further closures occurred during the nineteenth century, by 1900 it had revived and included some seven hundred monks and one hundred nuns. Expansion took place outwith Europe in the twentieth century, with new Charterhouses in North and South America and in Asia. Currently, the order has seventeen houses of monks and four of nuns. When it celebrated its nine hundredth anniversary, St John Paul II wrote to congratulate them, not so much for their longevity, but for their fidelity to their Rule: 'never reformed because never deformed' is their justifiably proud claim.

Important Carthusians

As with all religious orders, the founder is automatically its most important figure. St Bruno was born in Cologne, but spent most of his life at the great cathedral at Rheims. There, where the French kings were crowned and Church and monarchy met, he was master of the great cathedral school for no fewer than twenty long years. His role in the running of the cathedral was significant, and it was not until a severe conflict with the archbishop that Bruno stopped to consider his life. It was an interesting moment: a man who had actively served the Church was unreasonably forced out by a leading figure in that Church. His response was hallowed by time. When confronted by corruption in the Church there are two ways one can go: strive for reform of the structure, or remove oneself into the desert. The latter had been the solution in Egypt and Syria when monasticism was born, and it was to be the solution taken by St Bernard of Clairvaux.

St Bruno also opted for this road, but took one that led to an extreme form of monasticism. The Carthusian ideal is a severe one, but also one that has held perennial appeal for a small and dedicated group of men and women. Bruno himself forsook the life for many years, when called to service by Urban II. However, he never abandoned the vision completely, and ended his life in his second foundation at La Torre in Italy. To Bruno and his followers, the call of the Charterhouse is not primarily a call to flee the world, or the worldly Church, but one to a different type of service. It is a call for an individual relationship with the Divine, but also one to serve mankind through intercessory prayer. Indeed, this is at the very core of the monastic-contemplative life, and one to which the Carthusians devote more time than any other order in the Church.

The Carthusians offered another service to the Church, namely that of the written word. They produced a select and deeply influential group of monks and nuns whose writings made a very important contribution to the spiritual life outside the Charterhouse. Since the female component of the order has been a very important aspect of its existence, it is appropriate to start with Margaret d'Oingt, Prioress of Poletains Charterhouse (c. 1240-1310). In any other order,

Margaret would have been canonised, but the Carthusians believe in living saintly lives, not in creating saints. She is amongst the first group of French women from whom we have extant writings, using Latin in which she was highly competent, as well as Franco-Provençal. Her *Meditations* from 1286 are still consulted, amongst others by Benedict XVI. She also wrote a life of a rare Carthusian saint, Blessed Beatrice of Ornacieux. Her writings are marked by a strong sense of her own femininity, and it says much for the cross-gender appeal of St Bruno's spirituality and order that this is the case. Her writings show a deep passion for life, but for life as a road travelled to meet Jesus. It was a notion that has inspired many ever since.

Two Carthusian monks also made a deep impact on the spiritual life outside the Charterhouse. Ludolph of Saxony (1295-1377) wrote the *Life of Christ*, copies of which found their way into countless medieval libraries. Part of the so-called *Speculum* literature of the later Middle Ages, it was known as the *summa evangelica*, for it captures both the Gospels and Church teaching in easily understood and digested format. The end of the Middle Ages did not mean the end of the book's popularity: it has gone through almost ninety editions since 1474. Its meditation techniques were to inspire a huge number of saints, including the founder of the Jesuits, St Ignatius of Loyola.

The second major male author was Denis the Carthusian (1402-1471). He was a prolific author with over 150 titles to his name, and his great contribution was to distil much of the essential writings of the past fifteen hundred years. However, the most profound impact was his deep mysticism, which was a common element in the spiritual life of the Low Countries in his day, and which he popularised. Of course, mysticism, defined as a longing for God, is the essential characteristic of the Carthusian life.

Charism and Spirituality

One can do no better than quote the Carthusian Rule to illustrate the order's charism: "Christ, the Father's Word, has through the Holy Spirit, from the beginning chosen certain men, whom he willed to lead into solitude and unite to himself in intimate love". Solitude and love are the key principles of the Carthusian charism, coupled with silence. Now silence plays an important role in many monastic orders, especially in the reformed Cistercian or Trappist tradition. The silence of the Charterhouse, however, is of a different character: it is the silence of solitude, but of a positive solitude, one utilised to find communion with the Creator. Like the Cistercians, the Carthusians are deeply devoted to Our Lady. They use the Little Office of Our Lady in conjunction with the Liturgical Hours. Incidentally, they are the only religious order whose unique liturgy has been maintained unbroken since their foundation. Mary hovers over all that the order does, and the Carthusians played a major role in the development of the Rosary.

The Dominicans

During the twelfth century, there developed the ideal of the *vita apostolica*, the life of apostolic poverty. It was based on the description in *Acts of the Apostles* of Jesus's followers holding everything in common. Small groups of men and women lived in community, sharing resources and setting out to evangelise: their slogan was *non sibi soli vivere sed et aliis proficere*, 'not to live for themselves only, but to serve others'. The movement created many heretical sects, such as the Waldensians, as well as groups determined to work to restore the Church from within. These were to become a new movement within the religious life of the Church: the mendicants.

The mendicant orders devoted themselves to pure poverty, would not own property, either individually or communally. St Dominic, St Francis and the other early founders of the mendicant orders all begged for their bread, hence the name 'begging friars'. Later, this would be transmuted into a different form of begging, namely being paid to preach. It is interesting to note that different charismatic founders all came to the same solution to what they regarded as corruption in the Church, and did so independently from each other.

The rise of the Dominicans was astonishingly rapid. The young St Dominic had already shown a precocious interest in the poor as a student, when, in 1191, he had given away his possessions to the hungry during a famine. He later became a Canon Regular at Osma, following the Rule of St Augustine. The first time St Dominic began to develop an interest in preaching was when he accompanied Bishop Diego de Acebo of Osma on a diplomatic mission to Scandinavia. On their return to Spain, the pair encountered the Cathars. They believed in a duality in creation, with God and the devil being equally powerful. The evil one is responsible for the created world, which is, by implication, also evil. The human soul was a heavenly angel, trapped in the creation of the devil. To escape, the soul had to undergo a series of reincarnations, until perfection was reached. To achieve this, an unbelievably stringent set of requirements had to be met, including abstinence from many types of food and a renunciation of sexuality.

They tapped into local sentiment. The Languedoc was culturally and economically a highly-developed region, and its aristocratic leadership regarded the French king as an outsider. North of the Loire, many French aristocrats resented the independence of their southern counterparts, and the religious element gave shape to already sharply-drawn divisions. Both Bishop Diego and St Dominic were immediately drawn to the task of converting the Cathars. In 1205, the Pope approved of their mission, and a new form of religious life in the Church was born, that of apostolic preacher. Very early in 1206, the mission established a base at Prouille, where there was also a refuge for former Cathar women. It was to become the first Dominican house, both for friars and for nuns.

When Bishop Diego was ordered back to his diocese by the Pope later that year, St Dominic took over the mission. In 1214, he established a house in the city of Toulouse, the heart of the Languedoc, where his followers would live under the Rule of St Augustine, but in absolute poverty. Two years later, in December 1216, they received recognition from Rome.

The Dominicans soon became one of the most influential religious orders of the period, and, indeed, of all time. To date, they have produced no fewer than five popes, sixty-eight cardinals, eight patriarchs, 173 archbishops and 928 bishops. Their success was not the result of converting the Cathars: it was a task in which, in the main, they failed. However, their reputation as great preachers, great scholars and theologians, as well as their presence in the growing urban centres of Europe, soon gave them significant prominence. By the later thirteenth century Dominican houses were to be found all over Europe. Amongst their ranks the Domincans counted some of the greatest theologians the Church has ever produced: St Thomas Aquinas (1225-1274), St Albert the Great (1193-1280) and St Catherine of Siena (1347-1380) are all Doctors of the

Church. It also produced great mystics, such as Meister Eckhart (1260-1327) and, again, St Catherine of Siena.

The order survived the late Middle Ages with panache, introducing a restoration drive known as Observancy, which had many fruits. When the Reformation came, the circa twelve thousand Dominican friars were frequently the most successful of all in the defence of the Church. They played a key role at the Council of Trent, and, in the figure of Pope St Pius V, provided the greatest Pope of the Reformation period. Whereas many houses were lost in areas that became Protestant, the order expanded its reach in the missions. Dominicans played a leading role in the Americas, and were amongst the first to reach the New World, in 1510, and were active both in Latin America and in the north.

They had been active in Asia since the thirteenth century, which occasionally suffered set-backs after initial success. Thus, the Province of Persia (the order being organised in provinces) lost all fifteen of its houses in 1349. However, in most of the Middle East it persevered, and does so to this day. It has been present in Baghdad, Iraq, since the High Middle Ages. Dominicans were also active on the mission in India and in Cambodia, although their achievements there were eclipsed by subsequent missions of more modern orders.

Their active role in the missions and in the struggle with Protestantism made the Dominicans one of the most important orders of the Early Modern period. By the mid-seventeenth century, there were around 25,000 Dominicans worldwide around this time, spread across the globe, including Africa. Several suffered martyrdom, particularly in China, Vietnam and Japan.

They were hit hard by the gradual encroachment on religion and the religious life in the period that followed, culminating in the French Revolution and the Liberal suppressions of the nineteenth century. Provinces in Spain, France, Italy, Portugal and across Latin America were lost. For all the disasters that befell it, the order proved remarkably resilient: unlike most other religious orders, it managed to maintain a semblance of organisation, and it never fell below 3,500 friars. Its revival, then, began from a position of comparative strength. The nuns and sisters, too, recovered from a relatively secure base.

From the mid-nineteenth century onwards, the Dominican family recovered some of its position. Active provinces were erected, with particularly fruitful endeavours in France, Britain and the United States. The order reached a steady five thousand members, which it has maintained with a little fluctuation. Indeed, in several countries, notably Ireland, Britain and the United States, it has been disproportionally successful in terms of vocations. It provided a formidable contribution to the Second Vatican Council, and has been the theological bedrock of the Church in the modern period, as it was before.

Important Dominicans

St Dominic was born in Spain. We know little of his parents. He attended school and his reaction to poverty at the time has been mentioned above. Likewise, his careers as a canon and his early years in the Cathar mission have been mentioned. Once his new order received papal approval, he based himself in Rome, to be closer to the Papacy, but also to oversee the vital education of the brethren. He died, aged fifty-one, in 1221, appropriately enough, in the leading Italian university town of Bologna, where he had set a precedent by opening a Dominican friary specifically with an eye on the students.

Dominic lacks the heroic poverty, flamboyancy and charismatic features of his great contemporary, Francis of Assisi. He was described by a contemporary as "thin and of middle height. His face was handsome and somewhat fair. He had reddish hair and beard and beautiful eyes. ...His hands were long and fine and his voice pleasingly resonant." Behind this rather commonplace description was a man whose influence was enormous. Dominic almost singlehandedly ensured that the Church was to play a very significant role in the intellectual life of Europe, through the close association of his order with learning and the new universities. He offered a home to men and women whose intellectual curiosity could easily have led into heresy, and created a climate that allowed for questioning and reasoning. Unfortunately, although his order would be instrumental in codifying and promoting the devotion, he was not responsible for the Rosary.

It is impossible to offer even a short survey of all prominent Dominicans in the available space; those who follow are, therefore, representative. The first extraordinary Dominican is one of the order's Doctors of the Church, St Catherine of Siena, the co-patron saint of both Italy and Europe. Catherine was known as a very happy child, so much so, that she was called 'Euphrosyne', from the Greek for 'joy'. Her first vision was one of Jesus with Ss Peter, Paul and John. It was not so much the vision itself, as the fact that it came to an end that proved a burden on the child. Obviously, the vision of heaven made her instantly and acutely aware of the fallen state of the world.

From then on, St Catherine was destined to become a very special person. She frequently saw the saints and Jesus. This culminated, probably sometime during Lent of 1366, in what is known as a 'spiritual espousal'. This is frequently described in the language of a wedding, rings and white dresses included, but, as St Catherine acknowledged, words are not enough. The human being is 'lifted up to God', quite literally becomes one with Jesus in a similar way to which husband and wife combine to re-create the image of God in marriage.

St Catherine became a Dominican nun, and gained fame. She gathered a group of likeminded people around her, including Blessed Raymund of Capua, later the

Master-General of the Dominicans. In Siena, their deeds of mercy during outbreaks of plague, their fidelity, and, above all, their great skills in preaching, made them popular. St Catherine was one of the few medieval women granted a licence to preach. She worked for peace between the constantly warring Italian cities, and occasionally managed to get them to cease their warfare. More impressively still, she persuaded the Pope to abandon Avignon and return to Rome, bringing an end to the Avignon exile.

At least as famous as St Catherine, is the great Dominican artist, Blessed Fra Angelico (1395-1455). Born Guido di Pietro, he may serve as the outstanding example of the Dominicans' great contribution to the arts. The great Renaissance biographer of artists, Vasari, said of Fra Angelico that "it is impossible to bestow too much praise on this holy father, who was so humble and modest in all that he did and said, and whose pictures were painted with such facility and piety". He became a Dominican friar around 1423, and it says much for the order that he was encouraged to excel in his artistic work. His paintings in Florence and Rome are masterpieces of the Italian Renaissance, and helped bring about new linearity in the visual arts.

A mention should go to that fearless advocate of indigenous rights, Bartolomé de las Casas (1484-1566). A Spaniard, de las Casas became a Dominican in 1523. This was ironic, for as a young son of a colonist on

Hispaniola he had opposed the Dominicans for protecting the rights of the indigenous Indians. De las Casas found it increasingly difficult to ignore the atrocities carried out by Spanish settlers and Conquistadores. Indeed, he became the most vocal opponent of the cruelty of settlers and of the economic system imposed on the Indians. He travelled thousands of miles across South and Central America on their behalf, and crossed the Atlantic several times to petition the Spanish crown. Finally, he became the crown's most important adviser on what was then known as the East Indies, and proved a formidable advocate of indigenous rights until his death.

This list would not be complete without at least a brief mention of two of the greatest Dominican theologians: St Thomas Aquinas (1225-1274) and Yves Congar (1904-1995). Separated by centuries, the two men are symptomatic of what has made the Dominican order so special: a love of learning, great scholarship and outstanding communication skills. Congar was a Frenchman, whose theology was focused on the history and nature of the Church. Initially, his emphasis on ecumenical relations, reform and the promotion of lay involvement was resisted by the Vatican. However, his voice was instrumental in the Second Vatican Council, and St John Paul II made him a cardinal shortly before his death, aged ninety-one, in 1995.

St Thomas Aquinas hardly requires an introduction: such has been his influence that Thomism, the theological system named after him, has been the official theology of the Church during the twentieth century and beyond. In many respects, Thomas laid the foundations of the Church's teaching on such topics as natural law, ethics and metaphysics. His influence is all-embracing, hence his sobriquet of *Doctor Universalis*. Between them, St Thomas Aquinas and Yves Congar have put an indelible Dominican stamp on the contemporary Church.

Charism and Spirituality

The Dominican charism is one of learning and preaching, of study and communication. Much of this study has been directed, as seen above, at theology. However, there have been other, equally important elements in the order's charism. One of these is the notion of mystical union. We encountered this with St Catherine of Siena: the idea that the human being can find union with the Divine in the earthly life. This mysticism seems very far removed from the reasoned logic of Dominican life, but has been a persistent counterbalance to it.

There is an element of this contemplative Dominican strand contained within the Rosary, arguably their greatest practical contribution to the spiritual life of the Church. It also shows the Marian element to Dominican devotion, which was revisited by Yves Congar. Dominican Marian devotion derived in part from their long emphasis on charity and love. St Albert the Great, for example, taught that all humanity could experience God's love, the one tangible way to acquire positive knowledge of God. Underpinning the learning of the Dominicans is a great emphasis on meekness and charity, without which, they argue, it is impossible to gain real virtue.

The Franciscans

It is almost impossible to provide a short history of the Franciscans, as they are not so much an order as a movement. Like the Dominicans, the Franciscans originated in the ideal of the *vita apostolica*, the wish for a life of poverty lived for others. Again like the Dominicans, they owe their existence to one founder, an outstanding figure who perceived the needs of his society and acted upon what he saw. St Francis is one of the towering saints of the Church. He was the son of a very wealthy Italian merchant, and lived a dissolute lifestyle. A sudden conversion saw him stripping off his rich clothes in public, part of his total renunciation of every worldly value. Francis heard God's call to restore his Church. At first he believed this to have been a ruined church in the hills outside Assisi, but gradually he came to understand that he was destined to restore the whole Body of Christ.

His early years were lived out in the hills. By 1209, Francis had collected a group of followers around him, whose itinerant life of preaching and admonishing was sustained by begging. In that year, he wrote a first Rule for them. From the start there were suspicions in some circles about the 'Little Brothers', as they called themselves.

There was frequently little to distinguish them from the radical Waldensians, but the more prescient amongst the higher clergy realised that there was one, vital, difference. Francis stayed totally loyal to the Papacy, and never called into question key Catholic dogmas.

The most powerful of Francis's early supporters was the Benedictine, Cardinal Giovanni di San Paolo. This provides an interesting link with the Dominicans, for the cardinal had been the papal legate in southern France, where he had been involved in the struggle with the Cathars. He realised that, like the Dominicans, the Little Brothers were a Catholic answer to contemporary problems. His advocacy did much to persuade that greatest of medieval popes, Innocent III, to approve the first Franciscan Rule.

As early as 1219, the rapidly growing order faced internal dissension. This was to become one of the hallmarks of the movement that Francis started. The main question revolved around the way that the brothers should live their life of poverty. Whilst St Francis was alive, the various groups were bound to the order through his personal charism. This changed after he died in 1226. The *Zelanti*, who sought a strict interpretation of the rule of poverty, were opposed by Fra Elias of Cortona's group, who were more pragmatic. Interestingly, he had the constant support of Francis's very important female counterpart, St Clare of Assisi.

Not since St Benedict and St Scholastica had the Church witnessed such a powerful male-female partnership in the religious life. As a consequence, the Franciscan movement had, from the very start, a remarkably substantial female element. Since the nineteenth century, the Church has become used to having far more female religious than male. This was not the case in the Middle Ages. Although most orders and movements had female elements, it was only amongst the Benedictines that one can find a truly substantial body of female religious.

The prominence of St Clare ensured that for the Franciscans this was not the case. Deeply inspired by St Francis, Clare had become a religious against her father's expressed will. Originally, her community at San Damiano had formed part of a wider group of female religious, organised by Cardinal Ugolino, later Pope Gregory IX. However, the prestigious house at San Damiano soon dominated the other communities in the order, which within ten years of St Clare's death was named Poor Clares, after the woman who undoubtedly was its spiritual mother.

St Clare still enjoys a considerable reputation in spite of working closely with the most famous and popular saint of the Church. Unlike Francis, St Clare was a very competent organiser, under whose guiding hand the order spread rapidly. In light of her organisational skills, it is, perhaps, little wonder that Clare supported Fra Elias's group amongst the friars. It was Elias's vision for the order that prevailed. The order grew exponentially, and found itself in competition with the Dominicans in urban centres and at universities. Like their fellow friars, the Little Brothers soon produced some of the outstanding theologians of the Church, such as St Bonaventure, St Anthony of Padua and Blessed John Duns Scotus.

Nevertheless, divisions were never far away. A group of more extreme Franciscans, known as Spirituals, constantly strove for a more radical interpretation of Franciscan poverty. They were part of a wider movement amongst the Franciscans, usually referred to as *Fraticelli*. Almost all these groups would, in the long run, break with the Church. There is something deeply tragic in this. The main body of the Little Brothers realised that some adaptation of St Francis's Rule was necessary: they now found themselves in urban centres, at universities and in cultures very different from the rural and sometimes remote places where St Francis and his first followers lived. However, one can understand the frustration of the Spirituals, many of whom were inspired by Francis's earliest followers.

Several groups split from the main body, and founded orders, some of which were recognised by the Pope. These were rather numerous, and contained amongst their ranks the Celestines, approved in 1294 but supressed in 1317, and the Clareni, approved in 1474 and amalgamated with the Observants in 1568. This was but the beginning of a much wider fragmentation, usually inspired by young friars wishing to return to - or to restore, as they would have it - original poverty.

For the main body of the Friars Minor, as they were by now called, the great disputes of the thirteenth and fourteenth centuries resulted in a compromise, by which the order owned convents which procured incomes for its friars. It was from this that they were known as Conventuals. By the late fourteenth century, inspired by such luminaries as St John Capistran and St Bernardine of Siena, an Observant movement took root, wishing to restore a regular observancy of the Rule. They were frequently supported by local rulers, and, as with the Dominicans, formed separate provinces. In 1517, Pope Leo X ordered the division of the Franciscans into Observants, which he declared to be the real Franciscans, and Conventuals. Almost all the reformed Franciscan orders were amalgamated with the Observants, a process completed by St Pius V.

At the same time, the Poor Clares also divided into regular and observant groups. Founded and inspired by the remarkable St Colette of Corbie, a very strict reform movement returned many of the Poor Clare houses to total poverty. She enjoyed powerful patronage from French kings and Burgundian dukes, and especially from female aristocrats. Again, the decision was made to split the order, and, in 1448, the Pope recognised the Poor Clare Colettines as a separate order. They split further in 1538, when the Poor Clare Capuchins were established. This mirrored the development amongst the friars, for almost as soon as they were split into two orders, there arose a reform movement amongst the Observants. Founded in 1520, the Capuchins grew up as yet another attempt to recapture the original fervour of St Francis and his early followers. They, in turn, would split again. In Spain, several Franciscan orders sprang into existence, including the ultra-strict Alcantarines, whilst in France the important order of the Recollects was begun.

All this took place against the background of the Reformation, which saw vast numbers of Franciscan houses, and, indeed, whole provinces, wiped out. Nevertheless, the Reformation was not quite a disaster for the Franciscan movement. From the very start, they had been active in the missions, following in their founder's footsteps, as Francis had preached at the court of the Islamic ruler of Egypt. In the Middle East, in particular, but also in Islamic North Africa, Franciscans had long been active on the missions. This was recognised in 1342, when Pope Clement VI declared the Franciscans as the official custodians of the Holy Places, those parts of the Holy Land and the surrounding area sanctified in Salvific History. From the late fifteenth century onwards, Franciscan friars were active in the New World, where their contribution was greater than any other order. They also worked in Asia, but there were not as influential as the newly-founded Jesuits or the Dominicans. In Canada, the Recollects were particularly important, an importance recognised by the British after their conquest of Quebec, after which they expelled the order.

The eighteenth century was particularly cruel to the Franciscan movement. All over Europe and throughout the Americas, they fell victim to the hatred of the secularists, culminating in the devastation wrought by the French Revolution. Whole provinces vanished. One example will suffice to illustrate the severity of the impact: in France, all 2,534 Recollect friaries were closed, and the order effectively ceased to exist, except for some houses in the Low Countries. Elsewhere, numbers fell to precarious levels, and when Napoleon was finally exiled to St Helena in 1815, only a handful of houses and a few hundred Franciscan friars remained.

From that low, the movement recovered with remarkable success. This was helped in 1897, when Pope Leo XIII ordered the union of all Franciscan branches, except for the Conventuals, in one order. The Friars Minor reached a peak of 26,000 members in the 1960s, but has declined quite sharply since. The Conventuals, on the other hand, have increased quite strongly in the last few decades. In Poland, they are the major branch, whilst in Italy and the Philippines, too, they have a pronounced presence. They have been helped by the popularity of their main saint, Anthony of Padua, and by that of the great wartime Polish Conventual martyr, St Maximilian Kolbe.

Important Franciscans

As with all the orders, it is impossible to do justice here to the huge number of outstanding men and women who have worn the Franciscan habit. To date, the various branches of the Franciscan family have given the Church five popes, sixty cardinals, seven patriarchs, 291 archbishops and no fewer than 1,588 bishops. The two most outstanding individuals of the Franciscan family are its founding saints, Clare and Francis of Assisi. St Clare (1194-1253) is one of the most remarkable women in the Church's long history. The eldest daughter of a senior Roman noble family, she grew up in an environment of wealth and privilege. She had a precocious prayer life as a child, and in 1212, aged eighteen, after she heard St Francis preach the Lenten retreat in Assisi, she determined to embrace the religious life.

Clare's decision would be a bold one today, but in the context of her own age it was totally unheard of for a wealthy noble lady to embrace the type of life that she did. Cardinal Ugolino, the future Pope Gregory IX, clearly thought so too. In 1219 he gave the group of women that had joined Clare a Rule, based on that of St Benedict. Although Clare was satisfied with this in most respects, she did not approve of its provision for the ownership of property. It would seem that the cardinal had missed the essential point of St Clare's experiment.

What followed was even more audacious than Clare's original decision to become a religious: she defied the cardinal, even when he had become Pope, until he gave in and granted Clare her wish. Gregory realised that he was encountering a very special and deeply holy woman. Clare was marked by single-mindedness: subsequent to her retreat into the convent at San Damiano in 1212, she never left again. Such was her reputation that she was canonised in 1255, a mere three years after her death.

St Clare has been described as St Francis's rival in Christian perfection, and it has frequently been observed that nobody else was ever quite so Christ-like. It is difficult to write about St Francis (1181/2-1226) without using superlatives. He is easily the most popular saint in the Church. Part of his story was related above, and one cannot do more than provide just a few outlines here. As a young man, Francis was a drunk who attended parties, wore the most expensive clothes and generally did nothing but indulge himself. The conversion from this hedonistic life was total and gained him an instant reputation, both as a holy man, but also, in the view of others, a fool.

The story of the Cross of St Damiano speaking to Francis just prior to his total conversion is amongst the best-known in hagiography. Around 1208, after hearing the Gospel story of how Christ's disciples owned nothing but the barest minimum, Francis determined to embrace apostolic poverty. He had already attracted his first followers, and the original ecstasy of living this life of complete liberation from earthly attraction was to haunt the Franciscan movement for ever.

In the year 1212, Francis set another precedent for his followers: besides restoring the Church in Christendom, the Little Brothers would also work in the missions. By 1217, the order was large enough to be split into provinces; three years later there were some five thousand friars. At this point Francis relinquished control over the order, and was to live out his life as an icon of his Rule. Two years later, he conceived the idea of another iconic statement, the Christmas Crib, which Francis believed to be an excellent catechetical tool. By this time, although aged only forty-one, Francis's health was broken by his astounding asceticism. Always full of love for creation, he admitted on his deathbed that he had been over-harsh on his own body. He lingered on for some years, and died, consoled by the sacraments and lifted by the love of his followers.

The Franciscans have produced many significant men and women since Francis and Clare. Anthony of Padua, Bonaventure, Colette of Corbie, Agnes of Prague, John Duns Scotus, Peter of Alcantara, Pascal Babylon, Frederic Ozanam, King Louis IX of France, Maximilian Kolbe and many others all merit more attention than can be given here. They have left a distinctive, and distinctively Franciscan, imprint on the Church, have contributed to every field imaginable, from mysticism and Mariology to the social doctrine of the Church and notions of Christian leadership.

Charism and Spirituality

Much has already been stated about the essential charism of the Franciscans. Theirs is a total return to apostolic poverty, combined with a deep reverence for the created world. Over time, they, like the Dominicans, developed an intellectual tradition, and from the start they were fervent advocates of social justice. The main source for their charism lies in the various narratives around their great founder. St Bonaventure's *Legenda Major* is the official biography of Francis as far as his followers are concerned, but by far the most popular accounts are found in the *Fioretti* or *The Little Flowers of St Francis*. It has gone through more than sixty editions, is still in print, and gives the perfect insight into what has made Francis and the Franciscan charism so popular across the centuries.

The Carmelites

Of the main mendicant orders of the Middle Ages, the Carmelites stand out as being without a real founder. Indeed, even the dates of their foundation remain rather speculative. The order regarded itself as a continuation of an eremitical-contemplative tradition, which existed in unbroken succession on Mount Carmel in the Holy Land since the days of the prophet Elias. Indeed, that great prophet is regarded as the founder of the order. Few would now credit this. The first traceable record of men living what would become the Carmelite life dates from the 1150s, during the Crusader kingdom. In 1185, we read a report by a Greek monk called Phocas, that a Latin Christian from Calabria had assembled a small body of ten contemplatives around him on the mountain. They were living in a monastery close to the cave traditionally associated with Elias. That would imply that they already had a devotion to this great prophet, but the record is silent before this. Much ink was spilled in subsequent generations on the veracity of the Carmelite claim, so much so, that the Crusader origins of the order were neglected and lost.

There were some attempts to spread the order throughout the Latin principalities in the Middle East, but these soon floundered. Soon trouble arose around the proper form of life of the Mount Carmel hermits. The Patriarch of Jerusalem, Albert Avogrado (1149-1214), intervened, and around 1210 wrote a short Rule, based largely on that of St Augustine, which is unsurprising given that the Patriarch was an Augustinian Canon. The Rule, known as the Rule of St Albert, incorporated many aspects of the reform movements that had swept the religious life of the Church over the past few centuries.

Like the Carthusians or Camaldolese, the Carmelite brothers were to spend most of their days in their cells. There, they were to say the Office, meditate and pray. They were expected to attend daily Mass communally, and silence was to be the guiding principle of their life. In addition, they were to have no property. At first, this Rule appears to have been intended for just this one foundation on Mount Carmel. Besides the failed foundation already mentioned, new houses soon sprang up elsewhere in the Holy Land, in Acre, Jerusalem, Tyre, Tripoli and at an unknown location in Galilee. In all, there were fifteen Carmelite houses in the Crusader states. All of these were very short-lived, for they were founded as the armies of Islam were reconquering the lands they had lost to the First Crusade. In two of the houses, the brothers were martyred.

They tenaciously clung to their main foundation on Mount Carmel, and although they were frequently driven from there - all brothers were martyred in 1291, for example - they still had a large church on the mountain in the fifteenth century. For most of the brothers, however, life in the Holy Land had simply become too precarious. Soon, there were Carmelite foundations on Cyprus and Sicily. The earliest house in the West was in Marseille, but soon there were 'Carmels', as the houses of the order are known, all over Europe, with some of the earliest in England.

It was an English Carmelite, St Simon Stock (c. 1165-1265), who, upon his election as the Superior of the Carmelites in 1247, ensured that the order would survive the transition from the Holy Land to Europe. Many prelates refused to acknowledge the Carmelites' validity, arguing that they contravened the ban, issued in 1215 by the Fourth Lateran Council, on creating new orders in the Church. However, St Simon Stock managed to gain an interim approbation from Pope Innocent IV, and this sufficed until permanent approbation finally came at the Council of Lyons in 1274.

The English Carmelite saint did more than just gain legal recognition for his order. In 1247, the Pope allowed him to modify the Rule, reducing the period of silence and abandoning the solitary life for a communal one. They moved from being the *Eremitae Sancta Mariae de Monte Carmeli* to being the *Fratres Ordinis Beatissimae Virginis Mariae de Monte Carmeli*; they turned from being hermits into being mendicants. The order grew swiftly after this, and by 1400 had some 150 houses all over Europe. Many of these were, like the Dominicans and Franciscans, in university towns. However, there were always Carmelite houses in smaller locations as well, some even outside urban centres: the tension between their original, eremitical life and the mendicant life that they had adopted was to remain a significant factor in Carmelite life.

As the Middle Ages drew to a close, the Carmelites began to suffer from a similar decline in religious standards as all other orders. Restrictions on the ownership of personal property were relaxed, the rules of abstinence either ignored or modified, and even the communal life was no longer lived by many. Pride had a look in too, as Carmelites sought for high office in the Church. Like the Dominicans and Franciscans, the Carmelites also experienced attempts to return to a more rigorous observance of their Rule.

In Italy, what was effectively an Observant split occurred, with the Congregation of Mantua living a life much more closely conformed to the original Rule. It was to remain independent until after the French Revolution. In France, there existed a similar, but far more short-lived Congregation of Albi. However, the greatest reform movement came from Spain, and originated not with the friars but with the affiliated nuns. Again, the Carmelite family is unique amongst the mendicants for its very late development of a female second order. This did not begin until 1452, when the reforming Blessed John Soreth, founder of the Mantuan Congregation, began the first house of Carmelite nuns.

Even though they had been founded relatively recently, the nuns, too, had fallen away from a strict observance of the Rule. This created the environment in which two of the most significant saints of the Carmelites could introduce their reform. Both St Teresa of Avila (1515-1582) and St John of the Cross (1542-1591) were fervent reformers. They were also both very fine spiritual and mystical writers, whose impact on both Spanish and Catholic literature was enormous. Their theological and spiritual contributions to the Church have been recognised as outstanding, and both have been declared Doctors of the Church.

During their lifetime, both saints experienced much opposition: the vested interests within the order refused to see their comfortable lifestyles overturned. Inspired by St Peter of Alcantara, the Franciscan reformer, St Teresa had set out to reintroduce a proper observance of the Rule. She received sympathy, but little practical help, from the Spanish King, Philip II. However, with papal approval she founded a new Carmel, dedicated to living the Rule in all its strictness. Soon, she also founded houses for men, and there found support from St John of the Cross. Both saints were to suffer for their determined drive to reform.

St John was imprisoned and tortured, whilst St Teresa had to face the Inquisition. In the end, however, the two managed to drive through their reforms, and by the late

1580s a separate Carmelite order had come into existence, that of the Discalced Carmelites. Then, by 1600, a reform movement begun in Rennes spread throughout the Calced Carmelites, and all three orders thrived. From around the middle of the sixteenth until the latter part of the eighteenth centuries, the various parts of the Carmelite family flourished. The Reformation notwithstanding, it expanded rapidly, taking on a large part of the mission in the Spanish and Portuguese colonies, and providing many men and women in the struggle to re-establish the Church in parts lost to the Reformation. They even returned to the Holy Land, and, in 1631, re-established the house on Mount Carmel.

The nuns, too, experienced rapid expansion, particularly in France, where St Teresa's Carmel proved extremely attractive to women seeking the religious life. A curious footnote to that expansion is the fact that the order had several houses for English nuns on the Continent, mainly in what is now Belgium, whereas England had not known female Carmelites prior to the Reformation. All would be subject to the most violent repression. The English nuns managed to escape to Britain, but amongst the French nuns, a large group, known as the Martyrs of Compiègne, were guillotined. Numbers dwindled and did not really recover during the nineteenth century.

It was not until the 1880s that the Carmelite family experienced new growth. From a low of around 200 friars and around 250 nuns in all branches of the family, they grew to over 10,000 friars and many more nuns. This was in the late 1960s, after which there was a decline. Only the Discalced friars have managed to buck this trend, and now stand at an all-time peak of 6,700. That growth was not just in numbers; the order has provided the Church with outstanding figures, such as St Therese of Lisieux (1873-1897), St Edith Stein (1891-1942) Blessed Titus Brandsma (1881-1942) and Blessed Elizabeth of the Trinity (1880-1906).

Important Carmelites

In an order of many talents and considerable antiquity, the most important saint is a relatively recent one. St Therese of Lisieux, the Little Flower, is one of the most popular saints in the Church; to Pope St Pius X, she was "the greatest saint of our time". Her parents belonged to the 'petit bourgeoisie' and were known for their piety. All five daughters became nuns. Highly strung as a child, Therese showed a precocious love for prayer, but was frequently far from exemplary.

Aged four, she lost her mother to breast cancer. It affected Therese badly, and she became a withdrawn, rather serious child, tasked with looking after her younger sister. When she turned nine, her older sister, Pauline, entered the Carmel of Lisieux. From that moment onwards, Therese was determined to join her there. This longing intensified when, in 1886, another of her siblings, Marie, also entered the Carmel.

Christmas of 1886 was the turning-point in Therese's life. Already blessed with a vision of Our Lady, she had a vision of Jesus that caused her complete conversion. Now an adolescent, Therese showed a remarkable maturity: her desire to enter the Carmel was now based on a sincere desire to turn towards Christ, to live for him alone. This was confirmed by a pilgrimage to Italy, where she met Pope Leo XIII, and, in 1888, she received permission to become a postulant in the Lisieux Carmel.

The Lisieux Carmel had been founded in 1838, and had twenty-six religious when Therese entered. It was what was known as a 'petit-bourgeois convent', with a rather authoritarian, aristocratic prioress. The Rule was everything, as one would expect in a Discalced house, and Therese's fidelity to it was remarkable. As she grew in her vocation, her sense of her own 'littleness', her lack of importance grew, and liberated her. The suffering of her demented father, and her devotion to the suffering face of Christ, all deepened her union with the Divine.

Therese achieved a remarkable state of equanimity and love for others, so much so that the prioress said of her: "The angelic child is seventeen-and-a-half, with the sense of a 30-year-old, the religious perfection of an old and accomplished novice…she is a perfect nun". The 'perfect nun' felt anything but perfect, and continued to attempt to empty herself: the girl who had entered the Carmel wanting to become a saint had discovered insignificance, and, like St Francis of Assisi before her, became a saint. It allowed her to carry the awful pain of tuberculosis, from which she was to die, aged only twenty-four. The grace of her suffering, her beautiful modesty, her fine writings, including the spiritual classic, *The Story of a Soul*, all combine to make St Therese one of the most admired and loved saints of the Church.

With both St Teresa of Avila and St John of the Cross already briefly mentioned, we may finish this briefest of forays into the riches of the Carmel with a look at the saintly Titus Brandsma, the Dutch friar who was popularly known as 'The Professor'. Brandsma was the leading interpreter of medieval mysticism during the 1930s, and had been instrumental in the foundation of the Catholic University of Nijmegen, of which he was rector. His teaching career was one long attempt to balance Catholic teaching with the new world of Darwin and Marx. Above all, he was concerned that the Church was no longer reaching working class men and women. By the 1920s, his fame as a teacher, journalist and writer had reached national proportions.

As early as 1936, the Catholic Church in Holland had denounced Hitler as an anti-Christ, and had refused Sacraments to members of Holland's Nazi party, the NSB. Brandsma, too, had been denouncing the neo-pagans since 1935, focusing in particular on their anti-Semitism. When the Nazis invaded, he became a stalwart of the resistance. After his arrest early in 1942, in the wake of the Dutch episcopate's public denunciation of the Jewish transports, he was moved to Dachau. He was transported in a cattle cart on 16th May, receiving an illicit Blessed Sacrament from a German priest whilst standing in a station in Cleve. He arrived in Dachau on 19th June 1942. Already very ill, he was taken into the notorious Dachau infirmary, where medical experiments were the order of the day. He was killed by a lapsed Catholic nurse, who displayed a particular hatred for priests, and who injected him with a lethal poison. He was cremated the next day.

Charism and Spirituality

Two elements stand out in the charism of the Carmelites: their emphasis on silence and their devotion to the Mother of God. St Teresa of Avila, their greatest mystic, was succinct on Mary's importance to her, and her order: "May it be for the honour and glory of God, and the service of His most Blessed Mother, our Lady and Patroness, whose habit I wear." Of course, both are part of their great love for contemplation, so perfectly illustrated by St Therese of Lisieux.

Vocations

If the above has inspired you to enquire more deeply into the life and charism of any of the above orders, the following websites may be of interest. Vocations to the religious life, particularly in England and Wales, have increased dramatically in the past few years, reaching a total of sixty-four in 2012. In the USA, too, vocations are experiencing an upward trend. Elsewhere in the English-speaking western world, vocations are more sporadic, whilst in some parts of English-speaking Africa and in India they are at an all-time high. More ethnically diverse, more truly 'catholic' than in the past, the religious orders offer their members a life of total service and devotion, the opportunity to develop their particular gifts to the fullest and the chance to be part of the Church of the future.

General Vocations:

www.ukreligiouslife.org

cara.georgetown.edu/CARAResearch/Vocation_Fact_Sheet.pdf

www.religious-vocation.com

www.ukvocation.org

The Benedictines:

www.osb.org The Benedictine Confederation

www.benedictines.org.uk	The English Benedictine Congregation
www.monasterodicamaldoli.it	The Camaldolese Benedictines

The Cistercians:

www.ocist.org	The Cistercians of the Common Observance
www.ocso.org	The Cistercians of the Strict Observance, Trappists
www.vocationsplacement.org	Website for vocations to both the Benedictine and the Cistercian life

The Carthusians:

www.chartreux.org/en	The Carthusians
www.parkminster.org.uk	The Carthusians in Britain

The Augustinians:

This is but a sample of the many websites run by the widely branched Augustinian family

www.augustinians.net	The Augustinian Hermits
www.augustinians.org.uk	Augustinian Hermits in Britain
www.augustiniancanons.org	The Confederation of Augustinian Canons

www.premontre.org The Canons Regular of Prémontré (Norbertines)

www.servitefriars.org Servites in Britain

www.ursulines.co.uk Ursulines in Britain

The Dominicans:

www.op.org/en The Order of Preachers (Dominicans)

www.op.org/en The Dominicans in Britain

The Franciscans:

Again this is only a selection of the many websites of the Franciscan family

www.ofm.org The Franciscan Friars

www.friar.org The Franciscan Friars in Britain

www.ofmconv.net The Conventual Franciscans

www.thegreyfriars.org Conventual Franciscans in Britain

www.ofmcap.net/ofmcap The Capuchin Franciscans

The Carmelites:

www.ocarm.org The Carmelite Friars

www.carmelite.org The Carmelites in Britain

www.carmelite.com The Carmelite Family

www.carmelite.org.uk Discalced Carmelites in Britain